# Life's too Short

Foreword by Val McDermid

**BANTAM BOOKS**

LONDON • TORONTO • SYDNEY • AUCKLAND • JOHANNESBURG

TRANSWORLD PUBLISHERS
61–63 Uxbridge Road, London W5 5SA
A Random House Group Company
www.rbooks.co.uk

**LIFE'S TOO SHORT**
**BANTAM BOOK: 9780553825138**

First published in Great Britain
in 2010 by Bantam Books
an imprint of Transworld Publishers

Addresses for Random House Group Ltd companies outside the UK
can be found at: www.randomhouse.co.uk
The Random House Group Ltd Reg. No. 954009

The Random House Group Limited supports The Forest Stewardship
Council (FSC), the leading international forest certification
organisation. All our titles that are printed on Greenpeace approved
FSC certified paper carry the FSC logo. Our paper procurement policy
can be found at www.rbooks.co.uk/environment

306,36

Typeset in 12/16pt Stone Serif by
Falcon Oast Graphic Art Ltd.
Printed in the UK by CPI Cox & Wyman, Reading, RG1 8EX.

2 4 6 8 10 9 7 5 3

# Contents

# Foreword by Val McDermid

A long time ago, when I had a proper job, I was a newspaper reporter. I covered some pretty tough stories – the Lockerbie plane bombing and the Hillsborough football disaster among them. What saved me and all of my fellow reporters from buckling under the stress of the job was the feeling of solidarity we shared.

Last week, I heard that a former colleague of mine had died suddenly. I couldn't remember any details of the news stories we'd worked on together, but right away I could recall half a dozen funny stories about him. In turn, that made me remember a lot of other amusing things that had happened over the years.

I remembered Jack, who was maybe a bit too fond of a drink. He was having a company medical when the doctor asked, 'What do you drink?' Quick as a flash, Jack said, 'What have you got?'

Then there was the time I spent a week living undercover in a hamlet in the Yorkshire Dales. I had panicked because I couldn't find a single lead on the story I was meant to be digging up. At last, my news editor realized he'd sent me to the wrong village – I should have been in a place with the same name in Nottinghamshire!

And then there was the news editor I worked with when I was a trainee reporter. He acted as if our expenses came out of his own pocket. I was so poorly paid that I couldn't afford to run a car, so I had to go everywhere by bus. (Imagine trying to cover breaking news stories, like a warehouse fire or a bank robbery, when you have to get there by bus . . .) But my boss wouldn't accept so much as a claim for a 35p bus fare unless I had the ticket to prove I'd made the journey. You'd often see me and the other trainees rooting around on the floors of buses, looking for stray tickets that we might be able to use to squeeze a few more pennies out of the expenses system. With that early training, perhaps I should have been an MP . . .

So, while my memories of my old job do

include the actual work itself, what springs to mind first are the people I spent my days with. And that's what shines through in this collection of writing about life at work. The details of the jobs themselves are interesting, but what makes this book come alive are the relationships between the writers and those they come into contact with in the course of their work.

It's honest too. Nobody here is pretending their working life is perfect. But they're not whingeing about it either. They're telling it like it is, with all the problems and the pleasures, the frustrations and the fun. These accounts range from a bin man's adventures to life in British embassies abroad, but they all tell us something fresh about the world of work.

What these writers have in common, apart from their ability to paint a vivid picture of their working lives, is their involvement with their trade union. When I was a journalist, I was also a trade union official. Back then, we had the same goal as union officials have now: to make life better for our members. But our understanding of what that means has changed.

Back then, we focused on making life better only in terms of our pay and conditions. When we met the management for our annual talks, we discussed how big our pay rise would be and how large our expense allowances would grow. We would also see if we could reduce our working hours or increase our holidays and if we could improve the terms for redundancy. We only understood 'making life better' in material terms. It never occurred to us that we had a duty to do more.

But today, the trade union movement has found a new way to make life better for its members. Unions still fight for the jobs and the conditions of their members, but they've also found a new way to help them help themselves. Over the last ten years, a programme called unionlearn has encouraged members to develop their abilities, to learn new skills and to get formal qualifications.

Thanks to the learning and training chances the trade union movement has developed, members have moved up the career ladder faster and further than they dreamed possible. For many who were failed by the formal education system this has been the first time in their lives that anyone has taken the time to assess what they might be capable of and worked with them to attain that. People's lives have been transformed because someone gave them a second chance.

The Quick Reads programme has been one of the tools that have helped people on the journey to discovering what they might be capable of. There are all sorts of reasons why people leave school without basic reading skills. It might be a practical problem such as dyslexia, or problems at home. But people develop at different rates. Just because we fail at school doesn't mean we're doomed to failure for life. And that's where unions have learned to step in and provide a helping hand.

The authors who have written the pieces in this book have become part of that project. The stories they tell here are clear and direct. They make it clear that writing expressively is something we can all aspire to. Telling our stories is not just for a privileged few. With the right help at the right time, we can all find a way to share the events in our lives that matter to us.

The people who have let us into their lives through this book should be proud of what they've achieved. But what's just as important is that they've shown the way for readers and writers alike to follow. They show us what is possible. All we have to do is take the chance to follow them.

Val McDermid, March 2010

Val McDermid was born in Scotland and worked as a journalist for many years. She is now a full-time writer whose novels are worldwide bestsellers. They have been translated into thirty languages and have won a number of awards. Val lives in Cheshire and Northumberland.

# Don't Put Barney in the Bin Bag

## by Anthony Connolly

It was a cold winter's morning in the week before Christmas during the early nineties. As I arrived at the council depot, I noticed that the bin lorry I would be driving was frozen solid. I walked over, kicked the bumper and the keys fell to the ground. Having unlocked and forced open the frozen door, I climbed in and started the engine. Great, it worked, I thought. No need to hang around for the council mechanic to turn up four hours later and then tell me he'll 'need to go and get a couple of spanners to fix this, see you later.' I put the heaters on full blast, climbed out and trotted off to the canteen for a brew and some toast.

Like most council depots, the canteen was full of characters. I was working with Andy that week. He was the brains of any job he worked on, but he was always doing stupid things. He once went to a Christmas party and bit through some fairy lights. He thought it would be safe because the electricity was low-voltage. He found out it wasn't when it blew part of his lip off and gave him an irregular heartbeat. It had to be corrected by getting his heart stopped and started again.

The job we were doing that week was the Civic Amenity service. The service was free of charge. It allowed the public to get rid of bulky items that the bin men could not get in the lorry. These items included sofas, electrical white goods, televisions and, for some reason, garden waste. You must remember this was the early nineties. Recycling still meant going round the block on your bike twice.

Andy had been sitting in the canteen for about thirty minutes when I arrived. I was freezing. As usual, I said, 'Why didn't you start the lorry, lazy bollocks?' and, as usual, Andy replied, 'I've been up here sorting the work out.' Then, as usual, Mick butted in and told me to lay off him as he'd only had half a loaf of toast and three cups of tea.

The job was supposed to start at 7.30 a.m. We were meant to go around the area, collect about forty bulky items and take them to the tip. We used to get in early to sort out the truck and decide which pick-ups to do first. Then we'd usually leave the depot at around 8.15 a.m. Now this is when Andy really was the brains of the job – he was like a human satnav. He was able to remember every street in the area, and he would know the fastest way to get there, no matter what the time of day. The idea of multi pick-ups is to go to the furthest point first and then work your way back, but not for Andy. He was totally driven by money.

The pick-ups, you see, should be a maximum of three items per household, but if a customer were to offer enough money and ask if we could take a bit extra, then the sky was the limit. There was the in-between stuff that we just had to collect. Then there was the scrap metal that we'd always keep until the end for our own recycling purposes. This day's sort-out began, and our first job was to collect three bags of garden waste at the furthest point away. The next few jobs would be in-between items and then we'd go off to the tip.

The whole area was still frozen. The roads were OK because we had been out the night before, on overtime, gritting them. The winters then were tough. We would do our day job, then go and do a whole night's gritting. After that we went back to our day job. When we arrived at the first job, I noticed the three bags in the front garden covered in frost, waiting for collection. Andy, sensing a tip, stepped over the bags and knocked at the front door to ask where the bags were. I thought this was a good idea at the time, but it was really where all the trouble began.

The door opened to reveal a frantic, quite attractive lady, who was in her thirties. She looked quite confused to see two blokes in yellow coats standing in front of her.

'Yes?' she said quite abruptly.

'We're from the council,' I replied.

'We've come to collect your bags of garden waste, love,' Andy added in a sort of double-act way.

'Oh, er, there they are in the garden.'

'OK. Is this all you want us to take then?'

'Er, yes, if you don't mind.'

It was then I should have kept my big gob shut.

'Are you OK? You seem a bit upset.'

'Yes, I'm fine,' she replied, 'I've just had a bad start to the morning that's all.'

Then the look on her face suddenly changed, as though she had found the solution to her bad start to the morning.

'Can you take other things as well as garden rubbish, if I make it worth your while?'

Hearing this, Andy replied slowly, 'We're not really supposed to.' Then, speeding up like an excited kid, he added, 'But we'll have a look anyway.'

'Oh, well you had better come in then.' She beckoned us through the house towards a closed kitchen door. As we passed through the living room we saw about six kids. They ranged from around three to seven years in age. Two of them were on the couch and the rest were on the floor. They were all tucking in to what looked like jam on toast while watching the telly in front of the fire. As Andy and I followed their mum to the kitchen, we noticed they had all stopped eating. They were looking at us in total amazement. You know that wide-eyed, open-mouthed, face-covered-in-jam kind of look.

The woman was now calmer and less harassed-looking. She opened the kitchen door slightly and shoved us through, as though there was a secret inside. Then she closed the door behind us. We could hear her saying to the kids, 'Now listen. These men have come to fix something in the kitchen. If any of you come in just remember Santa is watching.' It was the usual threat that all kids get around this time of year. Then she slid herself through the door. Totally bemused I said, 'Well what is it then?'

Pointing to the corner of the kitchen she asked, 'Can you take Barney away for me?'

Barney? I thought. Who, or what, is Barney? Both Andy and I looked into the corner of the room. There he was, Barney the golden labrador. He wasn't barking or wagging his tail. Oh no, Barney was lying in the basket, on his back, with his legs in the air, as stiff as the frosted grass outside. Barney was the dead golden labrador this crafty woman had been trying to hide from the gang of pre-Christmas-energy-fuelled children in the next room.

'Well can you take him then?' she asked again.

'Oh, I don't know,' Andy replied.

'Look, if I give you twenty quid, will you take him?'

'Yep, not a problem,' Andy said suddenly with an unexpected change of heart. 'Ant, I'll go and get a bin bag and you get the back door open.'

'Hang on Andy, you can't put Barney in a bin bag!'

'OK, you sort out the back door and I'll go and get something.' Off he went, and I tried to open the back door to the garden.

'You can't take him out that way. There's no way round the front,' the lady told me.

'OK, well let's wait for him to get back and we'll sort it out from there.'

Andy came back a couple of minutes later with an old cloth sack that he had found on the back of the lorry.

'Will this do?' he asked.

'It's going to have to. We can't go through the back, though, so we'll have to take it through the living room. Let's get him in the sack.'

This is where the whole thing became quite difficult. Trying to show Barney a bit of dignity and shoving him in a cloth sack was quite a feat. Andy had hold of his head and I made the first attempt to get the bag over him, but I failed miserably.

'Give me a go,' Andy said. So Andy tried to get the bag on and failed. We were like Laurel and Hardy. The problem was the dog was so stiff we couldn't get his legs in the bag.

The threat of Santa had by now worn off. There were shouts of, 'Mum, can we come in?' Then there was banging on the door. I used this to our advantage.

'Look, love, do you want to go and sort the kids out while we do this?' I asked. So off she went, sliding through the smallest of gaps in the kitchen door.

'Right, let's get this in the bag and get out of here,' I said to Andy.

'But it doesn't fit.'

'Right, we'll just have to make it fit.' Thirty seconds later and 'there, it'll fit now'. So, it was in the bag for Barney and we were ready to go.

'OK,' we shouted through the door and operation get-the-f***-out-of-there began. Now Barney wasn't a small dog. In fact, Barney was a big fat dog. He weighed what felt like an eight-stone dead weight (pardon the pun).

Andy had hold of one end, I had the other, and off we went through the kitchen and into the living room.

It happened as we got into the living room, right in front of the kids. It's what they call sod's law. If anything is going to go wrong, it goes wrong at the wrong time, in the wrong place and in front of the wrong people. The bag split. It was not just a little tear that might have shown a bit of Barney's fur that no one would really notice. This was a proper rip.

You see, the brains of our little business had not only found a bag on the back of the truck, he had found a frozen-to-the-floor-bag. He had just ripped it up, obviously weakening it hugely. There was a thud and there he was. Barney was lying on the floor, dead, with broken legs. It was like one of those crashes on the telly where everything goes in slow motion, and then it all suddenly goes at a million miles an hour. The kids were crying and screaming, 'What happened to Barney?' The woman was shouting, 'Get it out of the house!' And Andy and I were flapping. Then the crash was over and a split second of clarity appeared.

'Quick, grab the dog, grab the bag and go!' I

shouted to Andy, who was standing at Barney's tail end. So that's what he did. He grabbed hold of the tail. Pull, snap and fall. Imagine the scene. Andy was now sitting on the floor about two feet away from Barney, with Barney's tail in his hand. The kids were kicking off big time now, and the woman was having a fit. 'Get up and grab its leg!' I shouted. He finally did and we were gone. Dog on the lorry, into the driving seat and off we went like a pair of bank robbers.

All day we wondered if the woman would ring the council and drop us in it. When we got back to the yard the manager was waiting for us. That was unusual. You never normally saw a manager after three thirty, unless you had some explaining to do.

I parked the lorry up and Andy jumped out to go and speak to him. When he returned he said, 'You know that job we had this morning?'

I thought, Here we go!

'Well,' Andy said, 'we forgot to pick the bags up. The woman has been on the phone to see if we can go back.'

We did go back, but we didn't knock that time.

# Life in the Fast Lane
## by Garry Pettitt

Anyone who, like me, has arrived at the tender age of seventy must have had, at some point in their life, at least one truly life-threatening experience. Or perhaps it's just one of those things you hear about that only happens to other people, like winning the lottery. I've known a major National Lotto winner, but I've never had any luck there myself.

My own scary experience, when I really believed I was about to die, happened on a very cold and frosty moonlit night in early December 1971. At the time I was employed as one of six long-distance lorry drivers. We worked five nights a week delivering twenty-one-ton bulk loads of coal to a large steel works at Port Talbot in South Wales. On the return journey we would call in at a coking plant at Bedwas, just outside Newport, to pick up a special type of hard coke. We would deliver this to metal foundries in the West Midlands. Then it was back to our depot in time for the day staff to take over.

The round trip was just under 400 miles. It took around ten hours at a time. This included all the tipping, loading, a couple of meal breaks and sometimes even a short nap! The route was mostly via motorways or good dual carriage-ways, and with very little traffic at night there were rarely any delays. It was, in fact, an ideal time to be driving a heavy goods vehicle.

We drivers used to stagger our departure times from the base. This was to minimize any waiting around to unload and reload in South Wales. On this particular night I had opted to be the last of our team to leave, so I left home at about 8 p.m. I was driving our newest lorry. It was a massive vehicle that weighed 32 tons gross. It was quite a mighty motor compared to our other five vehicles. It boasted an electrical device called the Telmar that prevented the lorry from going too fast. The Telmar assisted the braking, and therefore reduced wear to the brake linings.

To a young man of thirty-three, this was a

great lorry to drive. With its powerful, superb-sounding engine and its brilliant braking ability, it was almost a sports car!

After checking all the usual things, like documents, lights, wheels, tyres, water, oil and fuel, I climbed up into the cab. I roared off out of the depot towards the Strensham services area on the M5. It was seventy-five miles (or two hours) away and would be my first break.

At about 10.30 p.m., when I was suitably refreshed, I left the service area and turned onto the M50 for Ross-on-Wye. I noticed that the nearby fields were sparkling white with frost. It looked quite pretty in the bright moon-light. Rock salt had been sprayed onto the road earlier in the day by the gritting lorries. This prevented lethal black ice forming, so I was soon back up to maximum speed.

Leaving the end of the motorway at Ross, I took the A40 towards Cardiff and on to Port Talbot. The new M4 was being built at the time, but the stretch of dual carriageway we used was an excellent road. It had a few built-up round-abouts, and also a series of steep climbs and descents. After the slow hard pull up the hills, there was a tendency, without being too reckless, to go rather quickly down the other side. Occasionally I used the brakes and the Telmar speed controller. As there were mainly fields and very few houses beside the road, it was possible to see quite a distance ahead.

I was really enjoying the journey in the new lorry. The big Rolls Royce Eagle diesel sounded like a dream. It had just roared up a very long hill, a couple of gears higher than I was used to. The night was clear and bright and the cab was warm. My EverReady radio was playing Michael Holliday, singing about writing the story of his life. I was well on time, and all was well with the world. Man and machine in perfect harmony . . . until . . . I was shifting.

On starting downhill at around 60 mph, I could see that for some reason the moon's face was clearly reflected in the very shiny road surface. Suddenly uneasy, but still curious, I switched the Telmar to its first position. Nothing happened. About 500 yards away I could see a big roundabout rapidly getting nearer. Feeling really uneasy now, I switched the Telmar to its next position. Immediately, the engine stopped. The cab I was sitting in made an instant, even graceful, 120-degree turn to the right. I was staring along the side of the trailer, back in the direction from which I had just come! My worst fears were confirmed as I realized what was happening.

I had hit a stretch of the dreaded black ice. I was hurtling along sideways at 60 mph, jammed to the front of a trailer weighing 32 tons, completely out of control. My articulated lorry had jack-knifed, and although I had been driving such lorries for several years, I had never experienced this before. All those stories you hear about your entire life flashing before your eyes – I can tell you now that they are true. It happens so quickly, and in high definition!

Suddenly I was a very frightened young man. I realized that I was rapidly heading downhill towards a roundabout that I couldn't possibly avoid. Hitting it at speed would very likely overturn the vehicle, crush my cab and kill me. I didn't want to die. I was only thirty-three, with a gorgeous wife and a lovely little boy at home, and it was nearly Christmas. I wanted very much to see them again. I had yet to put up the tree and decorations for my precious little family, and I still had their presents to buy!

The roundabout was very nearly upon me. I clearly remember shouting some very strong language at the top of my voice. Recovering my senses, I started to dab the brake pedal on and off, on and off, on and off, quickly spinning the wheel to the left to steer in the direction of the skid. At the same time I tried to switch the Telmar retarder off. I even tried to push the starter button . . . just how many pairs of hands did I think I had? I really believed it was the end of the road for me.

Then, by some miracle, the cab just straightened up again. The stalled engine, which must have still been engaged in top gear, roared back into life. The wheels gripped nice, dry, ice-free tarmac. I was standing on the brakes as I entered the roundabout, thankfully at a greatly reduced speed. It was just slow enough to allow me to steer safely, if a bit sharply, around the built-up central island. Extremely relieved, I pulled into a lay-by just a few hundred yards further on. My fears gradually subsided, and I became aware of Michael Holliday, still singing about writing that story of his life.

It all happened within the space of a few

seconds. Nobody had witnessed it, and thankfully no other traffic had been around to get involved. It was several minutes before another truck came along. The driver stopped ahead of me in the lay-by and walked back to where I was standing. I had a cup of tea from my Thermos in my hands and I was trembling like a leaf, still thinking about my close encounter with death. In a strong Black Country accent, he advised me to be very careful on the way back, because there was a 'bit of black ice about'. He admired my nice new truck too. Still feeling rather bemused, I remember wondering how on earth he had managed to avoid having the same scary experience I'd just had. I didn't dare ask, but I shakily thanked him for his good advice.

After a few more minutes recovering from my fright, I made a close inspection of the vehicle. I was amazed to find that, apart from a wing mirror being out of alignment, there wasn't the slightest bit of damage. I had expected to find a big dent in the cab where it had been jammed against the trailer, but there was no sign at all that anything had happened.

It was over thirty-seven years ago, but most

of what happened in those few brief moments changed my outlook on life completely. Ever since, I've taken a great deal of care when out driving in any type of vehicle or weather. I even went to the extreme of taking, and passing, an advanced driving test in 1975 with the Institute of Advanced Motorists. I still hold a clean driving licence and remain a member of their worthy organization to this day.

I never did mention the incident to my wife. There was no reason to worry her with trivial subjects like jack-knifing and black ice now, was there?

# Riot

# by Frederick Creamer

I knew that something had gone seriously wrong when I heard the sirens. Were they ambulance, fire or police? The noise got closer and closer. I soon had my answer. I saw the police cars and vans roar by, sirens blaring and blue lights flashing. I told my fellow workers to stay by the barricades we had built and to make sure the security guards didn't remove the oil drums or wooden pallets. They had taken us up to an hour to place against the car factory gates. I then hurried along the edge of the factory wall to the other building, where I knew the police cars were heading.

As I got closer, I saw the night sky lit up by flames and the blue flashing lights of the police vehicles. I started to run towards the fire, sweating in the duffle coat I was wearing over my overalls. As I got closer, I saw that the store's depot was on fire. Directly in front of it, there were several bonfires made up of office furniture. All around there was what looked like snow carpeting the ground. I soon realized it was debris mixed with ash from the fire.

I heard excited shouting and laughter coming from above me, and I looked towards where the noise was coming from. About eight feet above me and to my right, a white china mug flew across the roadway and smashed into the office windows.

I stood transfixed as mugs rained down into the windows. More glass showered onto the roadway. The aim of the people throwing them was as good as a trained marksman, and they were putting out the remaining windows one by one.

Beyond the factory fence there were ranks of police. Their blue uniforms were lit up by their flashing lights and our flames. There must have been forty or fifty of them standing to attention. Their body language suggested they were ready to charge if given the order.

I ran up the concrete steps towards my fellow workers who were hurling the missiles. I reached them just as they were readying themselves to launch another barrage. 'Stop, stop!' I shouted. In my mind I was shouting, 'Cease fire, cease fire!' like an officer to his troops on the battlefield. 'What the fuck are you doing? Stop it!' They looked at me as if I was mad, but they stopped all the same. 'What the fuck's happened?' I shouted. 'We agreed to occupy the fucking plant, not burn it to the ground. You're destroying the place. Where do you think you're going to work once this is over?'

They looked at their feet, shuffling them. They were like children being told off by a teacher or parent. 'Can't you see the police for fuck's sake? They're just waiting for a chance to storm in and do us.'

Then I heard a crash and glass shattering. I turned round just in time to see a figure carrying a toilet bowl smash through the door of the managers' canteen. Then he carried the toilet bowl to the edge of the building. He lifted it above his head and hurled it down, shouting, 'Who wants a shit?' as he did so. The toilet bowl crashed through the windscreen of a car below, which happened to belong to a security officer, and ended up on the driver's seat.

If it wasn't a riot before, it was now. The barrage of missiles started again more viciously than before. A group of occupiers started to overturn British Telecom vans parked inside the plant. They tried to set them alight. I ran towards them, shouting for them to stop. Thank God they did. I then went to the men throwing mugs to get them to stop, which they did. Then I found that the arsonists had resumed their attempts to set the vans alight. And *then*, behind me, the throwers started up again. It was total and utter chaos!

I ran to the security lodge to find some of the other shop stewards. I wanted them to encourage their members to go to the main canteen for a mass meeting, in an attempt to stop the chaos. As I got close to the lodge, I saw one of the factory's senior managers. He screamed at me to get the men to stop. I tried to keep calm and said, 'Look, Peter, put them back on pay and I might be able to do something.' It probably wasn't the wisest thing to have said at that moment.

'You must be mad,' he shouted. 'We're launching the new model tomorrow. Stop them, just stop them!' It was only then that I noticed he was wearing striped pyjamas under his overcoat. Well, it was two in the morning.

While we were talking, or should I say shouting, more china mugs and large pieces of concrete rained down. They shattered as they hit the building and showered us with debris. Next to Peter was a rather large police officer standing silently like his men. The pips on his shoulders showed his high rank. His calmness in his perfectly neat, clean uniform was in stark contrast to the chaos going on around us. It was only when Peter stormed off shouting, 'It's madness, madness,' that I managed to speak to the officer.

'What do you intend to do?' I asked. He looked down his nose at me from under his shiny peaked cap, as if I was something he had trodden in. Then he surveyed the destruction going on around us and said very matter-of-factly, 'Nothing, nothing at all. If the problem is contained within the factory and it doesn't spread to the public highway, we will not interfere.' He then turned away and marched out of the factory.

Within minutes a loud noise came from the roadway. It was from a hand-held loud speaker.

A voice, which I instantly recognized as Peter's, blared out across the factory. 'We are launching the new model tomorrow. Stop what you are doing and get back to work. You are not only harming yourselves, but also the future of the plant. Please, please get back to work.' There was a pause in the men's actions as they thought about it, and then there was a roar as the rioters increased their momentum.

I went on searching and found as many shop stewards as I could. Then I led them, Pied-Piper fashion, towards the canteen. Between us, we managed to get most of the men together for a mass meeting. Instead of the heaving, screaming horde we had witnessed minutes before, now there were people lying on tables, exhausted from their efforts. This meeting was very quiet compared to the packed and angry meeting three hours earlier, when we had agreed to occupy the plant in the early hours of the morning in protest at the continuing lay-offs without pay.

The group was called to order and the crowd shuffled forward. Directly behind us, on the platform, was a brand-new car. It was the model being launched the next day. It was in show-room condition, untouched by the night's chaos. I looked at the men massed in front of us, and found it hard to believe that they were the same people who had been wreaking havoc only moments before. These men were responsible and hard working. They had families and commitments. They had been driven to these acts by their frustration at the company's indifference and its policy of laying off staff without pay or explanation.

The meeting was calm, eerily so. The senior shop steward explained that, if we workers were to make our point, we had to stop destroying the factory. It was our source of income. This was met with a silent acceptance. Our fellow workers agreed to the proposal to stay in the canteen until the morning shift arrived, when we would try to get the company to change their minds about laying off staff. As we said it, I thought to myself, 'No fucking chance'.

The occupation continued, but without the violence. The barricades were reinforced. Groups of men patrolled the plant, some on bicycles, to make sure the barricades were untouched and no more damage was done.

At about 6 a.m. Fred, a union official, phoned to say that he was coming to the plant to meet with us. I met him at the security lodge. As we walked across the roadway, our shoes crunched on broken glass and china. I said to him, 'Fred, you have got to support us on this issue.' He slowly looked around at the broken windows, the roadway covered in debris, the upturned British Telecom vans and the still smoking storeroom and just said, 'Fuck off.'

As a result of the actions that night, we were accused by the company of being anarchists, troublemakers and wreckers. One person was sacked. Five people were given various lengths of suspension from work without pay. Two shop stewards, including me, were given disciplinary letters for conduct unbecoming a shop steward. China mugs were replaced with plastic cups. However, new procedures were agreed between the company and the trade unions. They were designed to prevent any recurrence of that night, and we were never again laid off without pay.

# Life's Too Short
# by Francis Kenny

By the time you realize life's too short, it usually is.

It's funny but you never think about getting old when you're young. All you think about is what's going on that particular week. With work it was: How long is this job going to last? What's the next job going to be like? What are the fellas on the job like? What's the money like? Is the job easy? Hard? Clean? Dirty? You could never predict these things. Clean jobs might be well paid. And dirty jobs? . . . Well, the money might be crap. But what could you do? If there were no other jobs around, that was it: take it or leave it.

In the building game the saying was, 'If you're prepared to travel, you won't be out of work.' This was partly true. It was OK when you were young, but even then it wasn't great being out of town. Too many lads liked the ale more than the job. Too many of them made daft excuses to go on a half-day strike, just so that they could make a start on the ale. Flies in the toilet was one reason given for walking out at dinner time. Flies in the frigging toilet! What did they expect to find? Pink flamingos?!

Anyway, afternoon drinking didn't suit me. I'd go to the local pictures to watch a film, or go back to the digs to read a book. It was like that in the seventies, out of town on the big sites. Some lads chased the money, some were there for the ale and some were there for the women.

George walked past and gave a small wave with his *Daily Mirror*. He was in the building game as well. At fifty-five he's a bit older than me, but he looks more like sixty-five. He was a brick-layer. Bricklaying's a hard game. You're out in all weathers, except when there's a frost and the cement mix won't take. I'd only known George a short time, but he seemed a decent bloke. He was surprised when I told him what I did.

'A lagger,' he half shouted.

'It's a very important job putting lagging around pipes,' I replied jokingly, putting on a posh accent.

'A hairy arse lagger,' came George's response.

'And you're a hairy arse brickie,' was all I could think of to come back with. We both laughed and swapped stories, as you do.

It's amazing what a small world it is if you work in the same game. George knew fellas from the building trade that I hadn't heard of for years. We'd even worked on the same sites. Laggers never worked outside in all weather like brickies. You'd have to be daft to work out in all weather. Then again, what they earned was far from daft.

George had worked on some of the same jobs as me but not at the same time. He had worked on a job building a large extension at the Ford car plant in Halewood, which I'd also worked on later. I'll always remember that place. Not for the money, or the job, or for the fellas I worked with. None of that. I'll remember it for the football – and I wasn't even playing!

The new extension was large, over 200 feet long. My job was to fix metre-long fibreglass sections over the pipe work, then cut them to fit. I worked with an older lagger called Matty. Matty was old school to me. He was really old – at least forty – while I was seventeen. He liked to say, 'You never see an old lagger.' It was a common saying amongst laggers – well, the young and middle-aged ones anyway. You never did see an old lagger. The asbestos had got them. It caused two killer diseases called asbestosis and mesothelioma. Asbestos was banned in 1969. That was the year before I came into the game, so I never used it. It's mainly all fibreglass now.

So there we were. Matty was working on scaffolding and I was lagging the sprinkler system. And every day, there they were, right on the button for their twelve o'clock game of football. A dozen Ford production line workers would come into the empty building carrying a football.

They would take off their boiler suits while they were walking and put them down as goal posts. Then they got straight into the game. There was no kicking the ball about, no picking of sides, nothing like that. Right away they'd play the game. Then after an hour, when the buzzer sounded, they'd march back off to work. They'd put their boiler suits on as they returned to the production line.

Because the canteen was a ten-minute walk away, and because Ford didn't like us contractors using it, Matty and I would eat our sandwiches sitting on the scaffolding planks. Matty would read his paper while I watched the football.

The Ford men played like their lives depended on it. They were good, not great, but it was obvious they had all played a bit. I couldn't get over their commitment and enthusiasm. Their blue Ford T-shirts were stained with sweat after every game, even though it was in the middle of November. The teams' line-up would change every time they played, but they were always evenly matched. There were never more than a few goals in it. They took no prisoners either. At times they kicked the shite out of each other, but they never argued over decisions or fouls – except once.

A young bloke swerved past one of the other team and took the ball past a second older player. The older player took a few steps after him, swung a leg and caught the young fella under the knee. He flew three feet into the air as the ball carried on all on its own. One of the young player's team-mates shouted, 'Foul!' and stopped running. An older player shouted, 'Haven't got time for any of that lark,' and chased after the ball. The player who was kicked was already up and getting back into the game. And then the player who'd shouted for the foul ran as well.

I looked towards Matty. 'Did you see that?' Matty lowered his paper.

'That lad there,' I pointed, 'just got a right kick off him.' I pointed again. 'He sent him bleeding flying, but nobody said anything. No one did, well, one fella . . .'

'No, didn't see it, but what do you expect?' Matty went back to his paper. He couldn't be less interested, but it made a big impression on me. The way these guys just came out and played football and avoided any arguments said something about how working life ought to be. They worked hard and played hard.

A few weeks later I went back there to load the unused fibreglass onto the firm's lorry. By that time, the space that had been the five-a-side football pitch was covered with timber pallets. They were packed high with unpainted car doors, bonnets and side panels. Stacker trucks moved back and forth through corridors made of pallets and car parts.

George caught my eye by waving his newspaper. He was wearing his dressing gown. He pointed to the clock on the hospital wall with his rolled-up copy of the *Mirror*, gave me the thumbs-up and smiled. It's amazing how hardship brings people together.

Before, we had building work in common. Now we shared the nightly, along with the afternoon, ritual. The bed sheets were straightened. Waste bins were emptied and bedside cabinets cleared – regular as clockwork. It's funny because the clock rules visits too. People visiting come and go at regular times. Eileen and Holly arrive just past the hour and leave just before.

Eileen brings in something to eat. She always does, 'to keep your strength up'. Tonight she tells me not to eat after ten o'clock. The nurses tell you not to eat anything after twelve o'clock the night before. Eileen says ten 'just to make sure'. I knew she would go on about not eating after ten o'clock. Tomorrow is important. She says she'll be at mass when I'm in theatre. In the morning I'll go down on the trolley with an orderly. I'll make small talk about football or what was on the telly.

It's funny, or not so funny, how things work out. They ban asbestos and replace it with fibreglass. Asbestos can't be destroyed. It can't be burned or safely broken down. When it is broken down, it's into microns, a millionth of a metre. It gets into your chest and you can't get it out. So, they replace it with fibreglass, which can't be burned or safely broken down. Now it was in my chest and it wasn't coming out. Ah well, everyone's wise with hindsight. We'll see tomorrow.

By the time you realize life's too short, it usually is.

# Turn Right
# by K. Bryant

At the crossroads the policeman waves me through onto Riversby Lane. I am itching to slow the car and gawp. Surrounding the house on the corner, just before the turning into the school, are what seems like hundreds of armed police officers. They have black boots, bullet-proof vests, helmets and guns.

Some mornings I don't manage to make the next right turn into the school car park. Sometimes I keep driving and climb up onto the moors. I phone in with a migraine and sit on the heather in my suit, looking down on toy town Manchester. Today, however, I do make the turn. I double-check the car is locked and that nothing is left on the seats.

Brian, the caretaker, is raising the metal shutters from the classroom windows.

'Good morning Brian,' I say. I am a little too

loud and cheery, but the man is always rude, so I enjoy forcing him to at least say hello. He grunts a 'Morning' in reply.

James Hart ambles up beside me.

'All right, Miss?'

'Good morning, James.'

'Let us in with yeh.'

'You know I can't, James. Go on round the side.'

I aim for upbeat confidence, but James is six inches taller than me. If he kicks off, I'll have to stand outside the front door and wait until someone else arrives to help. I cannot let him in early with me. Goodness knows what he might break by the time the school day starts. James shrugs and climbs over the railings into the playground. The children at Riversby school can climb over nine-foot spiked fences as naturally as walking.

I wave my key pass at the sensor on the door. There's a contented 'clunk' as the electronic catch releases and I'm in. Mike, the assistant head of science, is loping across the entrance hall. He is stooping over a stack of exam papers – he is school exams officer, as well as being union rep, and health and safety officer, too.

'Hiya, boss.'

'Morning Mike. See the police?'

'Yeah, some armed siege at James Hart's place.'

'But . . .'

'I know, I saw him on my way in as well. He said he'd just walked out, no trouble. The police weren't after him.' Mike grins at me, the only-at-Riversby grin staff pass between each other.

As well as being head of science, I am a year-seven form tutor. I meet Sue, the head of year, every Monday to talk through ways we can help our pupils. At eight-thirty I run up the stairs to join the other four tutors in a class-room. Sue hands round some Quality Streets. She is very good at chocolates.

A face appears outside the window. It is Andy Chorley from year ten. He smiles and knocks, gesturing for us to open the catch. As he jumps in he nods matter-of-factly, 'Cheers Miss.'

He walks straight through the group of tutors, out the door and down the stairs. The only-at-Riversby grins melt into laughter.

As soon as the bell goes at eight-forty-five it's

downstairs to registration. Jack is first into the form room.

'I hate this fucking place.'

'It's a good job I'm deaf, isn't it, Jack? Good morning, Jack, nice to see you. Good morning, Miss, nice to see you too.' I like to role-play cheerful interchanges.

He rolls towards his desk and sits alone scowling. Since he started at Riversby, Jack has worked hard to make everyone dislike him. Maybe he finds it easier to deal with life if he is certain that the world is against him. Making friends is risky. He would have to deal with more hurt if the friendship went wrong. His mother has already abandoned him and run away to Blackpool. He doesn't want to take the chance of losing anyone else. I hang on to the hope that by helping him with his school life I might help him gain some self esteem. So, no matter how rude he is to me, he always gets a civil reply (even if I do end up talking to myself).

Harrison is sitting in the books cupboard, giggling. He does the same thing every morning and finds it funny. Jack leans on the door to stop Harry escaping. Suddenly Abbi is up on the tables, jumping across the desks like stepping stones towards Chantaine.

'Say that to my face,' she snarls.

I guide a laughing Chantaine out of the door before Abbi reaches her, close the door and stand by it. I face into the room, but keep my foot back as a wedge against the door, so that if it's charged I won't end up in casualty. Abbi knows the rules – she can't touch a teacher, so she can't get at Chantaine. I know Chantaine is bouncing up and down behind me. She is flicking Vs through the glass in the door, grinning through her sugar-melted front teeth.

Abbi yells swear words from the table. I look at her filthy trainers. Her mother is in prison and she is living with her grandfather. She has appeared this morning with a very short, wonky home-cut fringe.

A second face joins Chantaine's at the window. I slide through the door and raise my eyebrows at Kirsty, Chantaine's side-kick. Kirsty lives round the corner from school. She has to take her twenty-year-old sister's daughter to primary school, because her sister is in hospital with liver failure. Kirsty insists on hitching a lift back on an electric milk float.

'What can yeh do Miss? He was late, as usual.' She rolls her eyes and shakes her head in bafflement.

'Try walking?'

'It's just not possible, Miss, yeh know how it is.'

'You gonna let us in then, Karen?' Chantaine asks. I give her a level stare as both girls hug each other, giggling. They put their heads on one side and chime, 'Please, Miss, can we come in?' They fall onto each other again laughing.

'Promise to stop taunting Abbi?'

'Don't know what "taunting" means but yeah, we won't do it.'

My next class is with year ten, set three. Jordan makes a beeline for the back of the lab. His hands are below the bench before I finish the register. He bounces up and down gently, steadily, staring into the middle distance.

Louise and Bekki are laughing and throwing scraps of paper at each other. The paper had been Bekki's physics book. 'Girls! What are you doing?' I am upset that girls who are normally cooperative should do this.

'She deserved it.' Louise is smiling at her friend.

'Oh come on,' I say. 'What's she done to deserve that?'

'Her brother killed me uncle last night.'

A six-foot blond boy ambles into the classroom. 'Ian, out. You know you've been suspended.'

He looks right through me and sits down at the front, next to a quiet, shy girl. He snuggles up to her and pretends to read her work. Yasmin looks terrified.

'Ian, out.'

'Somebody say something?' He looks around with a mock puzzled look.

'Clare, go get Mr Morecambe for me please.'

Clare slips away down the corridor. Sometimes pupils refuse to fetch Kevin as they worry about the dangers of grassing. I glance up to check the camera is still up in the corner; its red light glows reassuringly. Ian starts to bang his hands on the desk, one, two, followed by a clap. One, two, clap. He starts to stamp his feet in time. The class, apart from Jordan, start to join in. It's like the opening of Queen's 'We Will Rock You'. I try to avoid crying. Mike appears at the door.

'Need some help here Miss?' he shouts.

The rhythm breaks and dies.

'Yes, she needs to stop pecking me head. She needs to learn how to fucking teach. I need an education to get a good job, and all she does is try to throw me out. I have a right to learn.' Ian is jabbing a finger towards me.

Mike lowers himself onto a lab stool next to Ian. Jordan is still gently bouncing.

Kevin walks in.

'All right Kevin.' Ian is friendly now.

Kevin is a doorman at some sticky clubs up town. During the day he is Riversby's bouncer. He also supplies pirated films and cheap bags of chocolates (only just past their sell-by date). He jerks his thumb over his shoulder.

'Out, now.'

'I would have gone if she'd asked me nicely.'

As Ian passes me, he says, 'Bitch,' under his breath. I can hear, but the cameras won't catch it. Ian is no longer allowed in my lessons because he keeps threatening me. He already has a criminal record for violence.

At ten o'clock, the bell goes and the children surge towards the door. A clatter draws my attention to Jordan, who is sprawling across the lino. The waist of his trousers is down at knee level. He looks up and round at his trousers, mystified. Picking himself up, he runs out clutching his clothes.

Georgina stays behind to help me pick up the exercise books, bits of snapped pencil, stools and paper. Guilt and frustration hammer at me. This girl deserves an education, and needs one to get out of her estate. How can I help her when I let these things happen in lessons? How can I change my teaching to stop it? I could do with time to have a good sob, catch my breath and get my emotions straight in front of the toilet mirror. But there's no chance. The pupils are barging in for the next lesson before Georgina has even left.

An hour later it is break. On a Monday it is my turn to stand at the fire door by the technology rooms, where I have to prevent pupils from ramming the door. I am also meant to stop any from heading upstairs. The base of the stairs, however, is five paces from the fire door, so I can only cover one or the other. I learnt in my first week at Riversby not to follow any children up the stairs as there could already be someone at the top, ready to land a gob of spit on my head. I tend to stand by the fire door and pretend I haven't seen the pupils rampaging up the stairs.

I peer through the wire-reinforced glass at the grey playground. The head of English is breaking up a fight. A group of year eights are legging it over the fence off to the chippy. There is a steady boom, boom, boom as some year elevens hoof a ball against the sports hall door. Anyone wanting to get into the playground from that side will be target practice for the footballers.

My second Monday duty is at lunchtime in the hall. Most children in the school are entitled to free school meals, but very few claim them. Last term I asked some year eights to write down what they had eaten that day. Only one child in a class of twenty-six had eaten any fruit or veg. A typical Riversby diet follows. Breakfast: nothing or a packet of crisps. Morning break: garlic bread and blue slush. Lunch: pizza with a can of Coke. Tea (if they bother to have any): chips with curry sauce and Sunny D. The pupils often miss tea as they spend most of the evenings out on the streets. Children in my tutor group draw me maps of the different gangs' areas. They explain the fights, the weapons they make, the police cars they attack for fun and the rubbish skips they set on fire.

Pizza crusts are flying across the hall. Harrison is throwing his lunch at some friends.

'Harry, pick up the pizza.'

'I didn't throw it, Miss.'

'I saw you.'

'You didn't.'

He starts to weave away.

'Harrison!'

A much older girl from year eight grabs him by the shoulders and steers him back to me.

'He's my uncle Miss.' She offers in explanation.

Turning him round, she instructs him to pick up the pizza. Harry refuses, so she picks him up. She turns him upside down until his nose is touching a pizza crust.

'Now fucking do it,' she instructs.

She carries Harry by the ankles and drops him into the blue bin. He is still clutching the pizza.

I have a free period in the afternoon and I head down the corridor towards the staffroom to empty my pigeon hole. Aimee, a bright, friendly year eleven girl with a poor attendance record, is crouching on the floor with her arms over her head.

'Aimee, you OK?'

'Miss don't look at me, don't talk to me.' She is panicking. I knock on the door of the head of the upper school to ask her for help. She tries to usher the girl into her office, but Aimee will only go in once the blinds are shut.

Yells come from the playground. The corridor windows seem to bow as they are thumped from the outside. Aimee hits the floor.

'You fucking bitch, get out here NOW.'

I call for Kevin. The man outside is Aimee's mother's boyfriend and a drug dealer. Aimee is more use to him on the streets bringing in money than at school. We are doing our best to help her stay in school and study for the exams that will get her to sixth form college. The police arrive to remove him from the premises.

As the bell rings for the end of the day, I am in my lab preparing for tomorrow's lessons when Georgina appears at the door and smiles.

'Milk and two sugars?'

'Yes please, Miss.'

Yasmin and Clare arrive and I add two more mugs to the tray.

For the next hour I teach them how a motor works. They listen, make notes and help each other to understand. They are preparing for the end-of-year exams and I give them a question from last year's exam paper. By ten past four they have answered the question. I show them the marking scheme, and enjoy watching as they realize they have got it all right. They thank me politely on their way out and I want to hug each one of them for their determination.

By five I have ground to a halt with marking and lesson preparation. The labs have darkened one by one as Brian lowers the shutters and locks them. I drift to the chairs in the prep room and offer the other science teachers a cup of tea. We sit comparing the day's events.

At half five Brian walks in.

'Haven't you cretins got homes to go to?' He turns off the lights.

'Hi, Brian. Have a nice evening.'

Mike walks out to the car park with me. I get in my car and lock the doors and then I drive out of the gates, turning right onto Riversby Lane. I like to keep my evening and morning routes different. A black police van passes on the other side of the road.

# The Other Side of Normal
# by John Morrison

## ME

I am me a human being
Caring touching feeling seeing
I may be different from all the others
Even from my sisters and brothers
I am me I feel the same
As others sneer, mumble and complain
Out of my way they do demand
Instead of stopping to understand
They call me cripple spastic and retard
From where others go I am barred
I am special you need to know
Why shouldn't I go where others can go
I may be different strange to see
But it's what's inside the real me
I am who I am I AM ME!
How much will it take to make you see
Look beyond this outer shell

Even when I scream and yell
To what's inside the real me
Trying struggling to break free
I AM ME!

The door to the bedroom swung open with a slow creak. It was a smell I'll never forget for the rest of my life. 'Don't worry, you'll get used to it,' the deputy told me with a smile. 'This is Charley. Say hello, Charley.'

I waited expectantly but there was no reply. 'Don't hold your breath, he doesn't talk. He used to, apparently, but then he just stopped. Since then he's never said a word. His parents are devastated.' The room was sparsely furnished. There was a bed, a wardrobe and a small chest. The floor was covered in lino, and the walls were painted eggshell blue.

'I know it's not very homely, but we can keep it cleaner this way,' the deputy said as she watched me look around the room.

Charley lay in his bed with the covers pulled up to his neck. He smiled, revealing toothless gums. Again, I was taken aback.

'He had all his teeth taken out when he was in the big house,' the deputy said. 'He was a biter.'

'Right,' was all I could say. He's not biting anything any more, I thought.

I could feel my stomach beginning to churn as the smell became more intense. It was enough to make your eyes water. 'Does he always smell like this in the morning?' I asked.

The deputy laughed. 'Don't be worrying yourself, you'll get used to it,' she repeated. 'Everyone has a problem at first, but you'll be all right in time.' She moved over to the wardrobe and took out some things for Charley's bath. She was very cheerful. This long-legged pretty girl of no more than twenty-six had worked in the profession for several years. It hadn't dimmed her good spirit. I guessed she must know what she was talking about and that, like she said, I'd get used to this.

She leaned over Charley. 'Ready to get up, handsome?' she said. 'He's my favourite. I know we are not supposed to, but I love him to bits. Got to have someone to care for you, right, bugger lugs?' She pulled back his sheet. He lay there naked with the beginnings of excitement for all to see.

I took a step back. 'Does he need a minute?' I asked.

'No, he's often like this. Aren't you, matey? Especially in the morning,' she said. 'He'll be fine when he gets himself up.' The sheet went on the floor and she pushed the wheelchair up to the bed, put the brakes on and laid a towel on the seat.

'Come on mate, it's time to get bathed and dressed. We let him get into his chair and do a few other things on his own. He'd let the staff do it all for him otherwise.'

'OK' I said. 'What do we do if he's not keen?'

'Don't help him, he can do this on his own,' she said with some authority. 'Some staff try to help him, but it's not in his care plan.'

I'd been working in this profession for just over a year. And what a year it had been. I'd learned how to clean up and feed both men and women, as well as deal with challenging behaviour. All without the training I thought we'd have. 'Learning on the job is what we do here.' That was my introduction to care!

My response was: What the fuck? No proper training? How do I know what a person needs or wants or what care to give? My last job had been in a very ordered environment and I'd thought this would be the same.

'Don't worry! You'll pick it up,' they laughed.

And so I had. It's strange how you develop a sixth sense. I now knew when to feed someone. I knew when to change someone, and when to duck and hide when it went wrong. The art of prediction had become second nature.

I learned how to understand people. It wasn't always easy, especially when the person couldn't talk to me in our supposed 'normal' way, or when they looked or behaved differently. I laugh now but, looking back, I made it up as I went along. I worried when I had to sleep over, in case I had problems with the people in my care and there was no one else to help. I worried about dealing with things on my own, and often that's exactly what happened.

I had read Charley's notes before I met him. He had been a healthy, active child who enjoyed running and playing outside, but he caught meningitis which had caused brain damage. It was then that his behaviour began to change. As he grew, it became more and more difficult to manage.

His parents had done their absolute best for him, with limited help and resources, even from professional services. But it had become too difficult for his mum and dad to continue to look after him at home. So, with much distress and regret, they had to let social services take him away and lock him out of sight in the 'big house'. There he was, yet another patient. He was a difficult one at that. He lived in a big dormitory with eleven others, none of whom he knew. Life was all about rigid routine and survival.

Lost and robbed of his sense of self, Charley loved to fight. Partly to secure his place in life, and partly to ensure he got attention from the staff. He was often jumped on by several burly male staff, sedated and put in isolation in a side room. Then he would try to escape by running through closed windows and doors. He caused damage and injury to himself and gave the staff some serious work to do. They bandaged him up and cleaned up the mess.

Then one day, so the story goes, he was taken upstairs by staff to a room on the second floor. Here he 'fell' through a plate-glass window onto concrete steps. He landed on his back. He was so badly injured he's been in a wheelchair ever since. I met with his parents often, and

They told me stories of how Charley had been as a child. They showed me photos of him in his cowboy hat, standing with his sister. He was full of smiles, mischief and adventure. He reminded me of myself when I was that age. My heart went out to his parents.

They told me how they regretted letting him go into the institution and how he had changed. They had sent in a healthy, fit, young man and got back a crippled, toothless shadow of his former self. His mum often cried and his dad looked away, unable to talk about it. The weight of guilt rested heavy on their shoulders.

Now Charley is part of the government's care in the community scheme. It's a shame they didn't have that scheme, and all the protection that goes with it, when he was younger. At least now we can offer him our support. We can protect him as much as possible from further harm.

Charley dragged himself out of bed, excrement everywhere. 'Doesn't he wear a pad?' I asked.

'He won't keep it on, so we have to help him this way,' the deputy said. She put on a plastic apron and gloves up to her elbows. I quickly followed her example. The bottom sheet ended up in a pile on the floor and Charley pushed himself away from his bed. 'We'll disinfect th all later including the floor. We'll bath hir first, though.'

'What do we do for him?' I asked. All th other people I'd cared for so far had been quit able. I'd done a bit of personal care, but neve on another man. I felt quite confident I coul manage though.

'First we shower him down, get all that o. him. Then he can have a soak in the bath. H likes bubbles, they help him relax. Then w need to do everything else.'

'OK, I can do all that,' I told her. I was happ that at least I knew how to bathe and shav him.

'Good, that'll be your job then. I'll get hi room and chair cleaned and ready. Then it wi be breakfast and we can chat about what h likes to do.'

I was so happy not having to deal with th smell again! I felt guilty knowing hov embarrassed he must be by it all. Charle grabbed my hand and guided me to push hir in his wheelchair. 'He wants to go to th bathroom,' the deputy said. 'He must like you.'

He smiled and we took him to the bathroom to shower him down and clean him up. Then I ran his bath and put the bubbles in. We hoisted him into his bath and he laughed.

'He sure likes that!' I said, glad that I was helping.

'Yep, just be careful he doesn't splash you,' he warned me.

I started to shave him and found it wasn't quite as easy as I'd thought. His face and head were covered in scars and marks. He had a boxer's nose, all signs of the knocks he had taken in life. Then I nicked him and there was blood everywhere. My face must have been a picture as he started to laugh. The deputy came in. 'Don't worry. It's hard not to cut him. Just look at him laughing at you,' she reassured me.

I stopped and looked at him. 'Got a wicked sense of humour, hey?' I asked.

'Don't let him fool you,' she warned. 'He's more aware than people give him credit for, and yes, he's got a very wicked sense of humour. He loves it when people do daft things or fall over. He laughs his head off.'

It was after a year of working in this sector that

it dawned on me that the people in my care wer no different to me. They just had differen difficulties to overcome, which resulted i different behaviour. Suddenly the bigoted, sc called 'normal' way of thinking left me. I stoppe thinking of 'them and us', as if 'they' wer different from 'me', and I started to realize hov important it is to accept people as individuals.

We went through the routine of finishin Charley's care, hoisting him up out of the bath drying and dressing him. Then we headed to the breakfast table. 'What you having Charley? the deputy asked. 'One day he'll shock us and tell us what he really wants, instead of u deciding for him,' she said. 'At least we knov he loves a cup of tea though.'

Charley grabbed my hand again. 'Looks lik he's taken to you,' she said, appearin; impressed. 'He don't usually take to people fo a few weeks. He likes to suss them out first.' Sh smiled at him, nodding and raising her eye brows. 'But don't get too complacent, he'll stil give you a thump if you get on his nerves.'

'I can't say I blame him,' I laughed.

I ate breakfast with Charley, helping him ea his food and drink, and so started our friendship

The friendship lasted beyond the time I worked with Charley, but sadly, due to my commitments, I couldn't see him that often. It's only now, many years later, as I look back on the time I spent with him, that I realize he actually taught me how to understand. He taught me not to pity, but to empathize with people with learning disabilities. He taught me to educate myself about different kinds of people. He taught me that we're all individuals and we're all different. Strangely, he also taught me about myself and my values and attitudes.

It would have been easy to treat him in the same way he'd been treated in the institution. After all, he was used to it. But, because I treated him as an individual, he became my friend as well as someone I supported in his life. I realized, through getting to know him, that he deserved to be treated like everyone else. I saw that he deserved the same freedom and access to life and all it has to offer, without fear of being stared at, talked about and verbally abused.

So what is the other side of normal? It isn't abnormal – it's that everyone is different. Everyone is an individual and we're all diverse.

All kinds of people make up this world of ours. It's just a shame that most people don't recognize that. How quickly we judge! How quickly we assume! How bigoted we really can be! Just stop for a moment and consider that this could have happened to you or to one of your family.

Some of the people I've met in the years since Charley weren't always the way they are today. Some had accidents as children, or suffered head injuries that created difficulties for them. Some had diseases that caused their current conditions, but for some society created the difficulties. When we don't accept diversity we can make life very hard.

In the past we locked up people who didn't fit – single mums, 'deviants' and anyone else we didn't think was 'normal'. So please, when you see someone different to you, whether they have learning disabilities, physical disabilities, or they just look different, don't judge! Don't be a bigot. They don't want your pity either. Just stop and say 'hello'. Maybe you'll get a smile and laughter the way I did.

# An Imaginary Letter
## by Esti Mardiani-Euers

Dear Genevieve,

From England I send my warmest wishes to you. They are as warm as the morning sun, as genuine as your smile! It's so nice imagining I'm sitting next to you on a peaceful and calm evening, far away from all my worries. Time has gone by and I've realized I haven't written to you since I came here. It's funny how life sometimes makes its own journey. We can never predict what will happen next year, month, tomorrow, or even in the next second.

I have always been tempted to write you a long letter, to tell you everything that has happened to me during the seven years I've been living in the UK, but I have never had the courage to do so. Mainly because I was afraid I would upset you, and there would be nothing you could do to help.

Now that seven years have passed I feel I am getting stronger. Somehow I have survived. Things look like they're improving, even though there is no guarantee as to what will happen in two years' time when I finish my studies. At the moment I am fine, so please don't worry about me. Just remember me in your prayers and hope that things will work out in the end.

Do you remember I once told you I wrote a novel? It was a love story, inspired by a secretary where I used to work. This young and eager lady fell in love with one of the consultants. He was a handsome, gentle civil engineer. But she had her heart broken, because he was a happily married man who already had two children.

My novel was only fiction, of course, but I imagined that this handsome man's wife had died and that the young lady gradually managed to build a relationship with him. I left the novel with an open ending so that I could write some more. Unfortunately, I never had the chance to continue with it. You should read it some time.

Anyway, to my surprise, several years after I

wrote that novel, a friend of mine introduced me to a white man from England. We stayed in touch and over time we fell in love. And this time it was a real story, not fiction. I married John and moved to the UK, and that's when life's adventures began. It was a big move, a big culture shock and an even bigger climate shock. One problem followed another.

While I was still in Indonesia preparing for the big move, sad news came from the UK. John had been involved in a serious car accident. A bunch of youths, who were driving wildly on the way to the pub, crashed into his car. He banged his head several times. He damaged his right eye and broke several bones. He became forgetful, which caused endless problems in his day-to-day life, but the worst thing was he couldn't walk properly any more.

I had been a university lecturer for more than fifteen years, and I had dreamed of doing a research degree in the UK. But now John needed too much care. I left Indonesia as soon as I could to look after John.

I had to wait a year before I could get a permanent visa to work. We lived a frugal life. I couldn't contact my sister in Indonesia, because we didn't have enough money to pay the phone bill, and I felt very lonely. Every time John and I went out, either to the hospital or to the doctor, we had to walk, because we couldn't afford the bus ticket.

Can you imagine having to walk in the cold winter weather? John was so unsteady that I had to hold him whenever he walked uphill. It really was hard work. What if he had fallen down? I would not have been able to help him up again. I am a small woman and I had to support a man who is six-feet tall.

The savings I had from Indonesia were running out, because I had to spend the money on food. Thank goodness there were charity shops where I could buy winter clothes and boots to keep me warm! I was so desperate. How on earth could someone with my knowledge, experience, skills and health not find a job to survive?

I kept saying to myself, 'I am a fighter, not a quitter!' I had to convince myself that this difficult time wouldn't last for ever, that there would come a point when things would get better. During my first four years in the UK I never stopped applying for jobs. Every week

I would apply for all kinds of job. I filled in application forms, wrote covering letters and updated my CV. Then I put them in the post or delivered them by hand.

Any job would do – casual, temporary, permanent, part-time, full-time. I would work as a general assistant in a grocery shop or restaurant, as a learning support assistant, teaching assistant, anything! And yet I could not find a job.

Very often my applications would get me an interview, but I would not get the job. There were always the usual reasons: 'We had a lot of candidates with higher qualifications, more experience.' I couldn't even get a job at the college teaching GCSE maths or numeracy level 1–2, and yet I was an engineer who used maths in my work every day.

I was frustrated, of course, and angry at the system. But life goes on and I had to survive. There was no choice. I had to keep applying for jobs until I got one. When we need to survive, we can be very creative. This simple and difficult life caused me to do something that I would never have done before. John's friend, Paul, suggested I go to adult education college to do an English course. I've always had an open mind when it comes to constructive advice, so I went there and met one of the tutors. She tested my English and told me I was between the intermediate and advanced level.

Unfortunately, at that time, the right course for me only took place in the evening. I couldn't do it, because it was winter and too cold and far for me to walk home in the evening. The tutor suggested instead that I do a Job Quest course. This is a course to help people who have just arrived in the UK to apply for jobs. It covered topics such as ICT, counselling, first aid, confidence building, communication skills, filling in application forms and interview techniques. I did the course and enjoyed it very much. It opened up a new world. I made some friends and was taught in a friendly environment. Most of my tutors were very nice and helpful.

In French, there is a proverb, 'after the rain comes good weather.' After eleven months of applying for three or four jobs a week, I got an interview for a job as learning support assistant at a young offenders' prison. Thanks to the Job

Quest course, I got the interview and I got the job!

I was so happy. For the first time since living in the UK I would have a regular income. I could buy bus tickets and proper meals. I even saved enough to buy a computer, so that I could email my friends in Indonesia as it's much cheaper than using the telephone. I decided to work half the week, because I wanted to do voluntary work at the adult college, as well as maybe some other courses.

But the saga was not over yet. After three months working at the prison, I realized that it wasn't the right place for me. It had a horrible bullying culture and I became a victim of this. I was verbally abused and threatened by the inmates. I was treated unfairly by the other staff and by my line manager. I can't really say more here, but somehow, for the sake of a stable income, I kept the job for four years, though every night I had nightmares.

After four years, however, I had to leave. Not because I resigned, but because the head of maths teaching changed all the maths classes at the prison to the afternoon. I taught at the adult college one afternoon each week, and this meant I had to choose. Either I would leave my horrible work place and lose my regular two and a half days' earnings a week. Or I would leave the adult college, a nice friendly environment, but where I only taught one session a week. But perhaps, if I stayed at the adult college, I could get more teaching hours.

It was a tough decision, but I decided to leave the prison job. I was afraid, of course, because it meant I didn't earn very much. But luck was on my side! Within a month of leaving there, I got to teach two new classes and gradually managed to build on that.

Life is not always gloomy if we can look on the bright side. I have always stayed positive. I have taken some other courses, such as watercolour, ICT, and teacher training. Gradually I've built up my teaching qualifications and my art skills. And guess what? Another surprise. I had my first watercolour exhibition at the Ashton Memorial in Lancaster. I also displayed my work at the Gregson Institute, and managed to sell some of my paintings. One of John's friends also paid me to do a painting.

I still wanted to do a research degree. I applied several times. I knew my chances were very small, but I might just be lucky one day.

Last July I taught three short courses and applied for an online learning course, I also met the supervisor of a research degree project in renewable energy – something I knew I would enjoy. I showed him my CV and some references I had from previous jobs. He seemed happy with everything and suggested I apply. After a month of restless waiting, I got the answer. I had won a scholarship. Hurray! I could return to university to do something I enjoyed very much.

If my research is successful, I will help this beautiful little planet by helping to develop green, eco-friendly energy. Mine might only be a small contribution, but by using carbon-free energy to make electricity, we can reduce our carbon footprint on earth. Hopefully we can save the planet for the next generation.

I still have to look after John. He hasn't been able to return to work because of his loss of balance, and he has to walk with a stick. He is fine at home, but going out always makes him panic. The damage to his right eye prevents him from telling whether people are moving towards him or away from him. This is a new world for him. He is often very angry and frustrated, and he has lost his confidence.

He used to be a fit, healthy man. He walked and cycled everywhere. He was doing a gardening job he liked very much. Now he can't do the things he liked to do before. I try to understand and put myself in his situation. This is a new challenge for me, too. I have to juggle my studies, work and looking after John. It is not easy. But what can I say? A friend once said to me, 'Take the world as it is, not as it should be.'

Let me close this letter with a good wish. May God bless us and always show us the way, so that we may do good deeds and care for other people to make this world a better place.

Please remember me in your prayers. Thank you for inspiring me with your genuine friendship, your support and encouragement.

Love from Esti

# A Brief History of Typing

## by Demelza Burrell

So, how did I end up being a Personal Assistant? By taking science A levels when I was to chemistry what George Bush is to the English language. I passed one A level in English, but the working world didn't really want failed A-level students, so I stumbled off to the local college to learn shorthand and touch-typing. This prepared me for my first job as a secretary in the Halifax Building Society.

Life in a branch of a building society was a gentle introduction to the working world. There was the customer who ranted at the cashiers behind the security glass. 'It's like talking to a goldfish bowl!' she would shout. And the transvestite who'd changed his name to Lady Friend, wore lipstick and had three days' worth of stubble.

There was the colleague who left one and

two pence pieces around the staff room to test our honesty. And another who alternated telling Mrs X about her savings balance with being Captain Kirk. He would start off with 'Captain's Log, stardate . . .' and often burst into song. And then there was the lovely manager who treated us all like we were family.

The best times were the comedy moments. Once my friend Nicky and I planted a rubber cockroach inside some mortgage files for a particularly unpleasant supervisor to find. It was very realistic. The file flew up into the air, powered by her pure horror. Bliss.

I also worked for a Welsh dragon who seemed determined to make everyone as miserable as she was. She lived off Slimfast and red wine, and had a vinegar personality to match. At the same time, I started to process loans under another supervisor, who was also female but very kind. It was like working under the good cop, bad cop routine. I'd spend half my time being told off by the Welsh dragon and the other half being beamed at by Brenda-the-Good-Witch.

I worked for the building society for four years, but there wasn't much scope for promotion. Some of my friends had moved away, so I began thinking about leaving too. I saw a job advertised in the newspaper, working for the Foreign and Commonwealth Office in London. It offered the chance to travel to those who had office experience. I knew I had to grab the chance while I was young and single, and I was amazed when I managed to get the job!

The move to London was a little bit of a culture shock, but the biggest surprise was the building I was working in. It was like a stately home, with never-ending staircases and corridors. It was made up of four different buildings, the Foreign Office, the India Office, the Colonial Office and the Home Office. They were all connected together at some point in the past, so there were some quirky floor plans.

Often someone popped their head around your office door to ask directions. I don't know many offices where, having worked there for several years, you would still come across things you hadn't seen before. Only recently I found a display cabinet, containing something that looked like the World-War-II Enigma code-breaking machine, in a random corridor I'd never been down before.

For such a beautiful building my first office was disappointing. It was like a Nissan hut. It was an extension on the very top floor with low ceilings, and it was unbearably hot in the summer. My new role was registry clerk, a job also known as office junior. I shared my office with two other people, both of whom were good-natured. One used to eat whole cakes for a snack, and make animal noises every time I blew my nose.

There was an older secretary in the department who used to order Berol pens in huge numbers, so we re-named her accordingly. We had a department head who came around every night to say goodnight. It was all very *The Waltons*.

We'd often be sent off with papers to take to a minister's office, and would find ourselves in a strange part of the building, unable to find the way there, let alone the route back! I felt that new entrants should be provided with a compass and a map with key points. You really wouldn't have been surprised to find Indiana Jones being chased by a large stone ball, or twins standing in the middle of a corridor with, 'Red rum, red rum,' pounding in your ears.

When it was time for me to apply for an overseas job, I decided I wanted to learn Spanish, so I applied for the three jobs on the list that were in Spanish-speaking countries – Cuba, Mexico and Spain. After an anxious wait, I found out I was off to Madrid in Spain.

When I first started my job in Madrid it was quite stressful. I had to learn a new role, and I had to get used to a different culture without friends and family for support. My work colleagues were wonderful. They invited me out, showed me the best shops and gave me helpful tips about living in Spain. With their help I survived my homesickness, but I ran up a large telephone bill from all the calls I made to my family and friends in the UK. It meant a lot to me when people at home took the time to record favourite TV programmes and send the videotapes to me. Spanish television wasn't very good, even once I started to understand it!

The embassy in Madrid was a rather ugly, grey building. It was circular, with a hole in the middle, like a concrete doughnut. Our ambassador used to enjoy rolling a 100-peseta coin as far as he could around the corridor towards my office.

He was an old-school diplomat. There was none of this 'Call me by my first name' stuff. It was 'Ambassador' and that was it. However, he did do you the favour of warning you when he was approaching by constantly singing. He wasn't fussy with his song choices either. It could be a hymn, a carol, a pop or a rock song. It was quite odd to see the normally stern-looking ambassador singing, 'It ain't what you do . . .'

As well as the quirky ambassador, we had a Dalmatian dog in the Embassy. The woman who owned him started bringing him into the office when he was ill, and then just carried on bringing him. It was funny to see the reactions of visitors when the lift opened to reveal a spotty dog.

There were also bats that would swoop over the swimming pool in the evenings, catching the various insects. They terrified one of our PAs who'd had a bat caught in her hair when she was a child. I always thought that was a myth, but she swore it was true.

I enjoyed my three years in Madrid, and got on pretty well with some of the local staff. I will always remember the black and white party I organized for everyone. I'd mentioned to one of the local staff that I was coming dressed as a maid, and I turned up on the night to find two of my very macho Spanish male colleagues had also come dressed as maids. They called me boss and followed me around all night – it was all very silly but good fun.

Soon it was time to apply for my next job. On the list was the job of Worldwide Floater. This seemed interesting. It would mean spending two years travelling the world covering job vacancies. You had no control over which country you would be sent to, and each job could last for three weeks or six months. It sounded like the ideal way to see places I might never get to see normally. Happily I got the job.

The first post was in Santiago, Chile, and I became friends with the two PAs there, a Scotsman and a Welsh girl. They would often link arms and catwalk model down the corridor towards my office. When we headed out for lunch, the Scotsman would swear that all the men were eyeing him up because of his blue eyes. He didn't seem to realize that he was walking next to a very pretty Welsh girl. She was the more likely object of their interest.

I was told that in Santiago there were coffee bars where businessmen could go and have a 'happy minute'. This involved the girls serving them taking their tops off for a minute! I'm still not sure if that was true.

In Santiago I experienced my first (and hopefully only) earthquake. I was asleep, dreaming that someone was shaking me. When I woke up I found the whole room shaking. I remembered the drill I had learned, and ran to the front door in my pyjamas to stand in the doorway. I was joined by my neighbour, who kept saying, 'Calm down, calm down,' in Spanish. It only lasted a few minutes, but it was the weirdest of sensations.

In total I visited twelve countries during those two years. Some of my adventures included being taken out dancing in Beijing to a club playing eighties tunes, which I later found out was a brothel. In Tehran I tasted my first curry pizza and enjoyed seeing the colourful parrots that lived around us – a pair had been released there years ago and they had since multiplied. They were a delight to watch, doing their Charlie Chaplin walks up and down branches and having arguments with each other.

In the Falkland Islands I remember the snowy walk from the guesthouse to Government House in the early morning, watching the sun rise over the water. One day after work I couldn't shut the door on my jeep because the locks had frozen, but I was soon rescued by the deputy governor and some anti-freeze spray.

In Freetown, Sierra Leone, there were the warnings about cobras, which kept me awake at night as I had nightmares about them slithering into my room. Much nicer were the giant snails. The security guards thought I was nuts when I went running off with my camera and a can of Coke to take a picture – well, with nothing to compare it with you have no idea how big the snail is!

When I was posted to Kazakhstan (pre-*Borat*) I had no idea where it was until I looked in an atlas and saw it was bigger than Europe! The local bakery there did a version of a pasty and a Chelsea bun, so I felt quite at home. It was strange, though, walking into a music store and finding a CD of Pam Ayres. The man in the shop informed me that the seventies band Smokie was very popular in Kazakhstan (work that one out!).

The receptionist at work there was a sweetheart with very much her own sense of style. She wore some pretty daring outfits. I was told that when Prince Charles was due to visit, she had been asked to tone down her clothes. She did this, but to add to the occasion, and in his honour, she dyed her hair blue.

Overall it was a great experience, but rather draining, and in the end I got tired of packing and unpacking. Every place meant a new job, new people and a new culture to get used to, and I was heavily dependent on the people I worked with for a social life. Some people made a real effort, but others left you alone to cope. At least, it made me more self-reliant and comfortable with my own company.

I was supposed to return to London next, but a job was advertised that needed someone quickly in New York, so I applied and got the job. I had always loved American music and film, and I'd dreamed of living there.

New York itself was everything you would expect. I'm not a *Sex and the City* girl, so I wasn't about to step out in designer shoes and go to the latest bar. My scene was most definitely the Lower East Side, with its dive bars and great music venues like The Bowery Ballroom and Mercury Lounge. I saw many fantastic concerts of many styles of music.

Work was hard with long hours, but I managed to find time to explore New York and some of the rest of the US. It's strange working somewhere where you constantly feel like you're in a film, waiting for De Niro or Pacino to step out of a bar, or seeing the steam rising from the manholes and yellow cabs all around.

My office building was about forty-five floors high. What they don't tell you is that when it's a windy day the building sways. The noise is incredible. It's just like being on board a ship with all the creaks and groans. I was sure it would topple over one day.

Working in a skyscraper meant we had a strict fire alarm routine. Every so often we'd have a fire drill and meet with the building supervisor, who would run through the plan. 'If there is a fire on your floor, please exit via the fire doors and, if it's safe to do so, re-enter two floors below.' Yeah, right, like I'm really going to re-enter a building that I know has a fire two floors above me. I prefer the option of going down the stairs and leaving the building!

The wildlife in New York consisted mainly of tiny dogs in handbags, rats and large cockroaches. Our office toilets would often have a couple of these black-shelled monsters lurking with intent. You'd sit on the loo and one would march out as if to say, 'Ha, caught you with your pants down!' Many a girl came screaming out of the loos with a cockroach scuttling behind.

I stayed in New York for four years in total and, after my posting ended, I had to return to London for my next job. Although sad to leave, I was glad to be coming home to my family and friends. I was looking forward to spending some time in my home country.

So now I'm back for three years, working in our main building in London. The creatures in this building tend to be mice rather than cockroaches. Recently a smell came wafting from the corner of our office, which could only be described as eau de dead thing. We were convinced it was a mouse who'd sampled the joys of our canteen, but the Rentokil man gave a sniff and said, 'not a mouse'.

He sprinkled some perfumed crystals over the area and left. So we now have eau de dead thing with floral hints. On that fragrant note I shall end. Learning to type has certainly led me through some strange and unexpected experiences!

# My Business Life
## by Bill Sutton

I was completely soaked by the lashing rain, and the water had started to trickle down the back of my collar. The heavy bag of newspapers cut into my shoulder, as I walked up the path to the next house on my delivery round. Why was I doing this? Definitely only for the money! Ten shillings a week would pay for an evening at the cinema and the latest Elvis Presley record.

I always offered to deliver any extra papers because my real dream was to save up and buy a motorbike, so that I could race around the block to impress the girls, just like the older lads. A pedal cycle somehow didn't have the same effect.

During the weekends and school holidays I was often asked to help in the newsagent's shop with simple tasks such as writing addresses on magazines for delivery, or filling the shelves with stock at busy times. My boss was an ex-Royal Navy man who had seen active service during the war. He was a good boss, firm and fair, and he had a good sense of humour. The rest of the staff were married ladies who either mothered or teased me!

When I was old enough to leave school, I wasn't sure what career to choose. In reality the choice was limited. Our generation was part of the baby boom after the war, and there was a lot of competition for jobs. At first I wanted to be an architect, but the thought of more years of studying put me off the idea, despite having been offered a place.

A local gents' tailor shop was advertising for a trainee, so I asked the owner of the newsagent's if he would write a reference for me. 'What do you want to be a tailor for? I've been waiting for you to ask me for a job!' he replied. So it was quite by accident that I started on my career as a newsagent.

When I arrived at the shop at six o'clock the following Monday morning, I didn't pick up a bag of newspapers and start on a delivery round. Instead it was my job to sort the rounds out for the other boys and girls. This didn't take too long because I had helped do it before.

'Right,' said my boss when I had finished, 'let's see if you can serve some customers.'

I was terrified. I had passed my O level maths, but it was completely different to stand behind a counter with a queue of customers rushing to catch the bus to work.

'Ten Woodbines, a packet of mints and a *Daily Sketch*,' my first customer demanded. To make matters worse, the cash register didn't add up the items for me. It all had to be worked out in my head. Mental arithmetic held no horrors for me in the classroom, but this was terrifying.

Somehow I struggled through the morning rush. Despite a few embarrassing moments when I gave people the wrong change, it was soon time for breakfast. I was allowed a long break at breakfast and lunchtime because I started work so early in the morning. The shop was open for twelve hours every day, and my day off was always during the week because the weekends were the busiest days. I was issued with a long grey overall, and had to wear a shirt and tie with smart trousers and polished shoes.

My boss was happy enough with my progress. He continued to train me in different tasks, including ordering stock for sale and setting out window displays. Eventually I was cashing up the money in the till at the end of the day and recording the sales figures. I was amazed to learn that we ordered Easter eggs in the autumn of the previous year, while Christmas goods had to be ordered in the spring!

After I had been working for a few months, my boss gave me a set of keys for the shop. 'I think you can open the shop on your own tomorrow. Just remember, if anything goes wrong, telephone me straight away. And don't lose them!' I felt like a real newsagent now.

My working life soon developed a pattern. Once the morning papers had been sent out for delivery and the staff had arrived, I was kept busy ordering goods, making window displays and dealing with customers' queries. After my lunch break, it was time to prepare for the evening newspaper rounds, before cashing up and closing the shop. My boss had bought another shop nearby, and I was given extra responsibility as he spent more time away.

Working in the newsagent's was a very sociable job, and it also gave me plenty of opportunity to meet the local girls. I had saved up enough money to buy a motorbike, but the problem was that I was at work when everyone else had Saturday and Sunday off, so I couldn't show it off! Luckily I was quite content to spend my day off working on my motorbike, fishing and exploring the local countryside.

In the shop we always made sure that we had a full range of magazines and newspapers available throughout the day. If supplies ran low, it was a great excuse to ride my motorbike to the local wholesalers. I could return with extra copies strapped to the pillion seat. As well as newspapers and magazines, we sold the favourite comics of that period. *Beano*, *Dandy*, *Bunty*, *Jackie* and *Topper* flew off the shelves in large numbers each week. If there was a free gift on the cover we always ordered extra to meet the demand.

The sweet department was heaven on earth. There were rows of glass jars filled with beautifully displayed fancy chocolates, and a large penny sweet section for the children who visited the shop on their way home from school. Salesmen from the different sweet manufacturers used to call. They carried large cases of samples to tempt us to buy their products, so I always made sure I tested as many as possible.

The following three years passed by very swiftly. One day a rather attractive young lady walked into the shop. She had the latest hairstyle, with ringlets piled on top of her head, beautiful make-up and a short pink mini-dress. It was only when she spoke that I realized she used to be a newspaper delivery girl. How time had changed her! The next time she visited the shop I asked her if she'd like to go to the cinema, and to my surprise she said yes!

One morning my boss called in to see me. 'Would you like to take over the position of manager at my shop on Daventry Road?' he asked.

'Yes, please,' I replied without hesitation.

I knew it would be challenging, but it gave me the chance to further my career. The move also meant an increase in my salary and a bonus scheme, which involved me meeting sales targets each year. The shop sold a much wider range of quality gifts, greetings cards and toys, as well as the newspapers and magazines I had sold before. At first my new customers weren't sure about me, but a friendly greeting soon broke down any barriers.

The shop also had a larger number of staff. They were all very capable and were a great help to me in the early days, but the task of organizing rotas, covering for holidays and working out their wages each week was a new challenge. It was never possible to please everyone! I would take into account their wishes whenever I could, but in return I expected loyalty and extra help when the business needed it.

Despite the unsociable hours my job demanded, love blossomed with my girlfriend. Pat had trained as a hairdresser when she left school, so she also worked on Saturdays. We had different days off during the week, but we were both free on Sunday afternoons. This gave us a chance to spend some time together.

On Monday, 14 February 1971, British money changed from the old pounds, shillings and pennies to the new decimal coinage. We now had one hundred new pence in the pound, instead of two hundred and forty old pennies. I had already attended a course at the local college in preparation for this, because it was the retailer's job to carry out the changes and educate the public at the same time.

After the shop had closed at lunchtime on Sunday, all the staff came to help with the massive task of marking all of the goods on sale with both the old and new prices. We also displayed conversion charts, so that everyone could check that we had converted the prices correctly. The changeover went fairly smoothly, although some customers complained that they didn't want those 'new coins'. For the first few days we accepted both old and new money, which made cashing up the tills interesting to say the least.

While my career progressed smoothly, Pat and I became engaged, and our wedding was arranged for June 1971. There was a flat above the shop available for us, so we began to clean it and make it into a comfortable home. By now I drove a Mini, so I sold my beloved motorbike to raise some money.

My boss called to see me one morning after breakfast. 'Bill, the manager of our shop in Winsford Avenue has decided to leave the company and we would like you to take his place,' he said.

This took me completely by surprise. I had worked at the Winsford Avenue shop when the manager had been on holiday, but it was on the other side of the city. 'I would like to take the position,' I replied, 'but I'll have to talk to Pat.'

After much discussion we decided to look at the living accommodation provided with the job. It turned out to be a large maisonette with three double bedrooms, all in good decorative order. This was a great start to our married life, but the accommodation was counted as part of my wages, and we would have to move out if I changed jobs.

After our honeymoon I had to set about getting to know my staff. It was a busy shop. I had hardly settled into my new routine before my boss decided to extend the premises and completely modernize the shop fittings. It was a real challenge to run a business in what was little more than a building site.

One morning my boss arrived early. 'Get your coat on, we're going to look at some shop fittings.' We visited factories and shops, even travelling as far as London before we found what we were looking for. The shop looked fantastic when the work was finished, and it attracted more customers, too.

The extra room allowed me to make attractive displays for Christmas, Valentine's Day, Father's Day, back-to-school, and all the other special times of the year. At Easter I filled the shop with massive pyramids of chocolate eggs. One particular lady came into the shop each year to look at the display. 'You will never sell all of those, Mr Sutton,' she would say sternly. Fortunately I proved her wrong every year.

'I would like to offer you the chance to become a director of the company,' my boss said when he called at the shop one morning. He went on to explain that, in return, I would train a new assistant manager and arrange for the other shops to be looked after when the managers were on holiday. I would be given the use of a company car, and get a bonus based on the profits made by the shops. It was a big responsibility, but I accepted immediately.

During the next few years Pat and I had three

children, a boy and two girls. The flat had plenty of room, but my boss was near retirement age and I suspected he might sell the shops. This would leave me without a job or a home. So we decided to buy a house nearby.

When I told him of our plans, he said that we shouldn't worry and that we would be looked after, but we still bought the house. It meant losing the free accommodation and starting to pay a mortgage, but somehow we struggled through.

Time passed very quickly. Running a business is a constant challenge. Some problems were easily solved. Others caused a certain amount of stress and worry, but the business continued to prosper. My boss did retire, as I had expected, but he made me a very generous proposition.

'I would like to give you the opportunity to buy the business', he said to me one day.

I was amazed, but told him I didn't have any money.

'Don't worry about that', he replied, 'I will arrange for the bank to lend you the money.'

How could I refuse? The thought of owing so much money was terrifying, but sales and profits went on improving. By keeping careful control of expenses, though, the debt was paid off in a few years.

The next eighteen years passed by in a blur. Our children had grown up into young adults, but the long hours and lack of holidays had begun to take their toll on us.

The news trade had changed and become much more demanding. The national lottery had been launched. This made it necessary to open later in the evening. Additionally, garages and supermarkets now sold newspapers and magazines. Fortunately, our shop was in a good trading position so, by sheer hard work and looking after our customers' needs, we continued to prosper.

One evening I was delivering papers, because the regular delivery boy hadn't turned up and nobody else was willing to help. The school children have so much pocket money now that they aren't interested in delivering newspapers.

I was completely soaked by the lashing rain, and water was trickling down the inside of my collar. It was then I realized that forty years as a newsagent was enough for anyone, including me. It was time to sell up, move on and start living my life.

People often ask if I miss the shop. The answer is not any more. Would I do it all again? I think I probably would!

# Merry Christmas Mrs Maud
# by Mick Neville

It was March 1988 when I found myself making one of the most important decisions I'd had to make during my sixteen years on the planet. The dilemma I faced was where I should start work. Should I look for an apprenticeship, or should I get a job at the big bakery where I had been working on Saturdays while still at school?

My mother was all for me getting an apprenticeship and learning a trade to secure my future, but my heart was lost to the local bakery, Fletcher's. It was a place where I'd already worked and knew lots of people.

Fletcher's was a great place to work, with a warm family feel. Mr Fletcher himself was the third-generation owner of this well-known Sheffield business. He looked after his workers, offering excellent pay and conditions. As a result he kept his staff for many years and gained the utmost respect among his 800-strong workforce. In the end I made up my mind that I would work at Fletcher's.

I left school on the Friday and, with not even a day's grace, started work at Fletcher's on the Saturday. It was a move from boyhood to manhood. I was suddenly surrounded by men with old-fashioned names like Leonard, Arthur and Ronald. These were names I'd never been familiar with before. Here I was, in their world, a world where you could swear in conversation without being told off. Men thirty or forty years my senior spoke to me with respect. It made me feel like I belonged. Up until then adults had always been teachers or parents, and I had always felt inferior to them.

The job I had come to do was elegantly titled 'Salesman's Assistant,' or in layman's terms, a 'van lad'. I worked on the vans, delivering bread and cakes to corner shops in the company of Rex, who was my allocated driver.

Rex had worked at Fletcher's for over thirty years, having started out as a van lad himself. He was definitely old school. He knew all the tricks and scams associated with the job, and was more than willing to pass them down to me as his apprentice (and maybe one day heir to his throne). Working with Rex was hilarious. He was so funny and could certainly tell a tale or two about the life of a bread man.

One particular frosty December morning in the middle of Mansfield, a very strange thing happened. We arrived outside Mrs Maud's corner shop at around 6.30 a.m. to find the shop lights on and the door ajar. Mrs Maud was an elderly lady of about eighty who always wore a flowery apron. She had run the shop for over sixty years, with her husband Wilf until his death, and on her own ever since. She was a lovely lady with a heart of gold, who always had kind things to say about everyone. Her shop's untidy shelves were stacked with everything you could ever want.

Each morning Mrs Maud would insist we have a cup of tea with her after we had stacked the shelves with bread and cakes. She would always give us something nice and neatly wrapped for our birthdays or Christmas. I can remember having the utmost respect for Mrs Maud. She reminded me of my grandmother – somewhat lonely. She always wanted to feed you and look after you as best as she could.

We always had to wait for her to open the shop. Rex would gently hoot the horn outside, and within five minutes or so she would appear to open up, dressed in her flowery apron, with the kettle furiously whistling away in the kitchen. However, this particular morning she was nowhere in sight.

We entered the shop. Rex called out to see if Mrs Maud was around. There was nothing, not a sound. This was very unusual, so he went into the kitchen to see if she was in there. Then he called me. As I entered the room I saw him reading a note that she'd left on the table. It read, 'Usual Please.' Also on the kitchen table were two cups of red-hot tea and Mrs Maud's flowery apron.

Rex and I looked at each other in a quizzical way. We began to glance around to see if we could see Mrs Maud. Maybe she'd gone out the back door to let the dog out? Or maybe she'd just gone back to bed? Either way, this was definitely out of character for her. We decided that she must have opened up the shop, made us a cup of tea and then gone back to bed without realizing she'd left the shop door open.

We filled the shelves with our bread and cakes as usual, and Rex made out the bill and left it by the till. Then we drank our tea, turned out the lights and made sure the shop door was securely fastened.

Rex started up the loud diesel engine of the bread van. This sent a choking plume of fumes towards me as I was putting the empty bread trays away. I closed the back door of the van and walked round to the cab. As I jumped into my seat I looked over my shoulder towards the shop and saw Mrs Maud standing behind the till waving to me.

'There she is, Rex.'

'Who's there?'

'Mrs Maud. She must have come downstairs just as we were leaving,' I said.

'Oh well, we'll catch her tomorrow,' he replied.

The rest of the day carried on as normal. We went from one shop to another, sometimes drinking tea, stopping at the chippy for dinner and laughing most of the way. Rex's sense of humour was so dry. He would have you in stitches with the way he told a story or a joke.

For me, this was the difference between

school and work. I was now in the adult world. I was working with people who were much funnier than any comedian I'd ever heard on the radio or seen on television. That's what made my job so enjoyable. I couldn't believe that, at sixteen years old, I was getting a huge sixty-five pounds a week for doing something I loved.

Finally we went back to Fletcher's, removed the empty trays and washed the van. Then we filled it with diesel for the next day and parked up in our parking slot. My job was to brush out the back of the van while Rex went into the office to pay in the day's takings.

Once the van had been cleaned inside and out, I had to fetch the confectionery for the next day. As I waited in line for my journey number to be called out, the smell of warm apple pies, custard tarts and sausage rolls made my stomach rumble. These delightful items were carefully passed through the serving hatch for me to carry to our van. Rex would always return from the office with a freshly baked loaf for me to take home to my mum. He'd say, 'Don't be late in the morning!' Not that I ever was.

On this particular day, however, he returned with a loaf for me but with an unusual look on his face, one that I had never seen before. It was a look of worry or concern. 'Come on,' he said, 'I'll give you a lift home.'

On the way home in the car, he told me that a strange thing had happened while he was paying in his cash. One of the supervisors had asked him to go to his office after he had cashed in and placed his order for the following day. In the office the supervisor began to question Rex about how many shops he had the keys to. In those days it was common for a bread man to have the keys. This meant they could let themselves in at unearthly hours of the morning and fill the shelves with fresh goods.

Rex told the supervisor how many shop keys he had and assured him that the customers were all very happy for him to have them. The supervisor then told Rex that Mrs Maud's daughter had phoned in, and that she hadn't known that Rex had keys to her mother's shop.

Rex told him that he didn't have keys to Mrs Maud's shop. He didn't need them as she was always more or less up when we arrived. Rex asked the supervisor if something was wrong with Mrs Maud's daughter, and whether something had been taken from the shop. He explained that the door of the shop had been ajar when we'd arrived that morning, so anything could have been taken by someone entering from the street.

The supervisor was a little confused as to what Mrs Maud's daughter's concerns were. He told Rex she wanted to speak to him tomorrow when he arrived at her mother's shop.

The next day, Rex and I carried out our normal day-to-day duties, but I had this nagging feeling at the back of my mind about the confusion the day before. Rex didn't seem himself. He was unusually quiet and I couldn't help wondering if he thought I'd taken something from Mrs Maud's shop. I had to ask him.

'Rex, you don't think I took anything from Mrs Maud's shop do you?'

'God, no!' he exclaimed, 'I would never have thought that of you in a million years, Mick, but something isn't right, mate.'

We arrived at Mrs Maud's shop bang on time to find the lights on and the door locked. There were some Christmas decorations in the window, and a Christmas tree. It was surrounded by the fake spray-on snow that usually takes until Easter to remove. I can remember looking at the window and smiling to myself, and thinking how hard Mrs Maud must have worked to get the display looking so nice. It was a massive achievement for a lady of her age, but it was typical of her to enjoy and share her Christmas spirit with everyone.

I gently tapped on the shop door to alert Mrs Maud to our arrival. The door of the kitchen opened and I saw Mrs Maud's daughter approaching. I looked at Rex and could see that he was thinking the same as me – this was something that had never happened before. She opened the door and welcomed us in with a 'good morning' and a smile. On the counter, two cups of tea were waiting for us and two neatly wrapped Christmas presents, one for me and one for Rex.

Cynthia, Mrs Maud's daughter, passed us the presents and said, 'My mother bought you both these Christmas presents for being so kind and looking after her.'

'But it's two weeks until Christmas,' I said.

'Where is Mrs Maud, Cynthia?' asked Rex.

'She passed away yesterday morning at 4 a.m. That's why I had to ring the bakery,' she said. 'I couldn't understand how you managed to get in. The shop was all locked up and we were all up at the hospital.'

Rex explained to her that the shop door was open when we arrived, and that we had thought it was strange. He told her that we had looked for her mother and, when we couldn't find her, we had filled the shelves and made sure the shop door was securely fastened.

Cynthia explained that she had trimmed up the window out of respect for what her mother would have wanted. She thanked Rex for locking up the shop, and told us both how much her mother respected us. She said her mother always looked forward to seeing us every day for a cup of tea and a chat. We both said how sorry we were and thanked her for the gifts.

But what about the cups of tea that were there for us yesterday, the flowery apron, the note that was left, and the fact that I saw Mrs Maud as Rex drove off? I couldn't bring myself to mention it, and neither could Rex.

\* \* \*

Time has passed by so quickly. I still work at Fletcher's Bakery, not as a van lad, may I add, but as a trainer in the bakery itself. Fletcher's has seen many challenging times over the past twenty years, but the attitude of the workforce hasn't changed. We are still very much a family concern. We will always look out for each other. We are 'Fletcherized' and there's no getting away from it. It's a quality we should thank the Fletcher family for and be proud of.

I believe the qualities we share at Fletcher's are the same qualities Mrs Maud could see in Rex and me all those years ago. Sometimes just the smallest acts of kindness are the most valuable. Taking time with people and being respectful of them can prove priceless. Mrs Maud valued Rex and me. I read that note, drank that tea, saw the flowery apron and I definitely saw Mrs Maud wave. I now understand it was to be her last goodbye. That's respect.

I never got the chance to say it then, but I would like to put the record straight now. Thank you very much and Merry Christmas, Mrs Maud. God bless.

# Quick Reads

## Books in the Quick Reads series

| | |
|---|---|
| 101 Ways to get your Child to Read | Patience Thomson |
| All These Lonely People | Gervase Phinn |
| Black-Eyed Devils | Catrin Collier |
| Buster Fleabags | Rolf Harris |
| The Cave | Kate Mosse |
| Chickenfeed | Minette Walters |
| Cleanskin | Val McDermid |
| A Cool Head | Ian Rankin |
| Danny Wallace and the Centre of the Universe | Danny Wallace |
| The Dare | John Boyne |
| Doctor Who: Code of the Krillitanes | Justin Richards |
| Doctor Who: I Am a Dalek | Gareth Roberts |
| Doctor Who: Made of Steel | Terrance Dicks |
| Doctor Who: Revenge of the Judoon | Terrance Dicks |
| Doctor Who: The Sontaran Games | Jacqueline Rayner |
| Dragons' Den: Your Road to Success | |
| A Dream Come True | Maureen Lee |
| Girl on the Platform | Josephine Cox |
| The Grey Man | Andy McNab |
| The Hardest Test | Scott Quinnell |
| Hell Island | Matthew Reilly |
| Hello Mum | Bernardine Evaristo |
| How to Change Your Life in 7 Steps | John Bird |
| Humble Pie | Gordon Ramsay |
| Last Night Another Soldier… | Andy McNab |
| Life's New Hurdles | Colin Jackson |
| Life's Too Short | Val McDermid, Editor |
| Lily | Adèle Geras |
| Money Magic | Alvin Hall |
| One Good Turn | Chris Ryan |
| The Perfect Holiday | Cathy Kelly |
| The Perfect Murder | Peter James |
| RaW Voices: True Stories of Hardship | Vanessa Feltz |

| Reaching for the Stars | Lola Jaye |
| Reading My Arse! | Ricky Tomlinson |
| Star Sullivan | Maeve Binchy |
| The Sun Book of Short Stories | |
| Survive the Worst and Aim for the Best | Kerry Katona |
| The 10 Keys to Success | John Bird |
| The Tannery | Sherrie Hewson |
| Traitors of the Tower | Alison Weir |
| Twenty Tales from the War Zone | John Simpson |
| We Won the Lottery | Danny Buckland |

# Quick Reads

## Short, sharp shots of entertainment

As fast and furious as an action film. As thrilling as a theme park ride. Quick Reads are short sharp shots of entertainment – brilliantly written books by bestselling authors and celebrities. Whether you're an avid reader who wants a quick fix or haven't picked up a book since school, sit back, relax and let Quick Reads inspire you.

We would like to thank all our partners in the Quick Reads project for their help and support:

Arts Council England
The Department for Business, Innovation and Skills
NIACE
unionlearn
National Book Tokens
The Reading Agency
National Literacy Trust
Welsh Books Council
Basic Skills Cymru, Welsh Assembly Government
The Big Plus Scotland
DELNI
NALA

Quick Reads would also like to thank the Department for Business, Innovation and Skills; Arts Council England and World Book Day for their sponsorship and NIACE for their outreach work.

Quick Reads is a World Book Day initiative.
www.quickreads.org.uk                    www.worldbookday.com

# Other resources

Free courses are available for anyone who wants to develop their skills. You can attend the courses in your local area. If you'd like to find out more, phone 0800 66 0800.

A list of books for new readers can be found on www.firstchoicebooks.org.uk or at your local library.

Publishers Barrington Stoke (www.barringtonstoke.co.uk) and New Island (www.newisland.ie) also provide books for new readers.

The BBC runs an adult basic skills campaign. See www.bbc.co.uk/raw.

www.quickreads.org.uk          www.worldbookday.com